Endless Desert

Michael Martinez

Endless Desert
by Michael Martinez

Copyright 2019 Michael Martinez
All Rights Reserved

All Music and Lyrics in this book are Copyright 2019 Michael Martinez

ISBN 978-1-7337939-0-2
Published by Michael Martinez
PO Box 64324, Sunnyvale CA 94088

Printed on demand starting 02/2019

This volume contains a series of poems (lyrics) that I have written with the intention of making them into songs and eventually recording and releasing those songs. I have completed writing the music for the first several of these poems, you will find these as lead sheets. I intend to record these as an EP titled "Golden Twilight". The rest of the poems appear in text format as I have not completed the music for them yet. I intend to convert these into songs at a later date.

Arranging and recording "Golden Twilight" is currently in progress, mostly finished, and hopefully I can finalize and release those tracks soon. If and when I do, those will be available on sites like cdbaby and soundcloud with the titles of the songs as given in this book.

The best way to describe the type of music is a combination of new-wave goth, jazz-pop, and singer-songwriter. Perhaps an appropriate term could be "philoso-pop" as many of the songs are heavy on philospohy.

First and foremost my goal in writing these is personal artistic fulfillment - the expression of things that I have left mostly unexpressed up to this point during my life.

A note about the music. The lyrics to most of the songs are sung with syncopation and anticipation of the beat. I have tried to notate this by using eighth-notes on the "and" ("&") but in some cases it's more of a triplet, in other cases a sixteenth, and I haven't been consistent about the notation. The best thing is to feel it out, knowing that it shouldn't be sung with straight eighths. You'll be able to hear the proper phrasing on the sound recordings, if and when those are released.

The song "Grey Skies and Blue Waters" has the subtitle "Laurie's Dolphin Tattoo"

Michael Martinez
mwtzzz@gmail.com

Graciousness and Empathy

every day this journey
was in my thoughts
every day I prepared
a little more
thinking how you would like it
thinking how it would bring you joy
Fine details didn't escape me
little last minute lists so i wouldn't forget
I wanted clear blue skies and clear blue waters
a picture perfect portrait of repose
in my mind rehearsed
moments of happiness
witty conversations
acute observations
silent passages of mutual nearness
giving you space when you needed it
at just the right time
i went out of my way to do these things

Tiger Somersaults

This thing always comes between us
I don't know how to get past it
it's a thorn in my side
I can't get past it
it consumes my waking moments
then I forget about it
but it returns to haunt my dreams
It's a cruel thing
You want more than love
I need love more than anything
Half a solution
But we each see only our quarter
Moments we giggle and throw tiger somersaults
your smile precious as I toss you high
tiger somersaults in the air
in the thickets you'll find a pot of honey
in the dresser drawer a bracelet of dark stones
on the mantle a small bear
in unchanging repose
observing with his mysterious dark eyes
Then you leave
you forget me in a broken state
short term memory is too short
i'm just a plaything
You taunt me because you don't care
but I know you really care
somewhere inside
some things are just a different matter :
you say mine are too
I don't know what we can do
We leave eachother
We return again
Looking to possess our quarter love
like an alchemist turning slight love
ever and always hopeful
ever and always knowing
Moments we giggle and throw tiger somersaults
your smile precious as I toss you high
tiger somersaults in the air
in the thickets you'll find a pot of honey

in the dresser drawer a bracelet of dark stones
on the mantle in unchanging repose
a small bear observing with his mysterious dark eyes

How It's Gonna Be

I call you up
I get worried
cuz you don't respond

Is it too early
are you busy

I call you up
I get worried
cuz you don't respond

Are you out
are you angry

Are you playing games with me
Is this how it's gonna be

i'm waiting
for any little sign

Are you playing games with me
Is this how it's gonna be

i'm waiting
for any little sign

The Unceasing Crackling Just Below the Level of Audibility

just this side of nothingness
coming through the black starry sky
an unceasing hammer strikes a concrete foundation
snug in my hammock
listening to faraway busy sounds
coming through the gentle blowing wind
a star is a white pinhole
which the other side
is spontaneous combustion
out of nothingness
snug in my hammock
contemplating secret things

The Forever Lament (II)

on a bright summer's day
playing games in the schoolyard
under the clear desert sky
tools of conviviality

good nature and concessions
we have a lot of patience
shared feelings of an endless horizon of beauty
for the length of our lives.

The feeling does not last
a new kid arrives
the harmony that was shared
falls apart
with motives surreptitious
whether by design or nature

treacherous hand working meticulously
its true nature you cannot see
treacherous hand working meticulously
its true nature you cannot see

toil under threat of punishment
or toil under carrot
either way at the end they've got you
Fantine is lost to history
the promise of some light
at the end of the tunnel
nobody recognizes the mask
ultimately this lopsided scenario
never amounts to any good
for anyone

if you knew the real reasons
would you agree to it
not how it should be
but is how it is

seemingly innocent excursions
to the countryside

have revealed desirable assets
then a song and dance
about why we need to make war

it's all a lie
an insidious sickness
like an oil spill or gangrene
you won the hearts of my friends
as you started to rob them
of their spirit

to claim divine providence is the ultimate deception
to assuage an oil spill as it poisons the sea
the social condemnation
which artificially creates hell on earth

all these things are hidden beneath our feet
since the foundation of the world.

Beacons

13th century passage
checkered spires in the bright blue sky
a great stone bridge solid as a fortress
immobile in the autumn air
contorted faces
aware of their fateful places
grimacing in wicked delight
the wide river stretches
driven forward, cannot change it
predisposed under the austere black testaments

a chill night air
tramway wheels squeeking
blaring sirens and bus fumes
stone faced and dry people
immobile on the sidewalk

in the park you are talking with your friends
a question of orientation
your slim body leans forward
your young face earnest
your hand trembles in your haste to be helpful

thank you so much take care
radiance in the land of despair

–

In the land of Todi
rolling hills gentle through ancient farmlands
a winding road through a stone archway
narrow cobblestone road in twilight
as dusk nears
small arched passageways into alleys
with single lamps hanging low
pale yellow lights on doorways

between stone balconies
into a jewelry shop
your long black hair
your easy smile

your unassuming character
almost as if you weren't there
nobody pays attention to you
except me

My companions are looking at the wares
I tag along with indifference
I sneak glances at you
You meet my gazes with your gentle smile

You'll Love Me Forever

I don't need to ask you why
You'll love me forever
There is no reason why
You'll love me forever

All is Forgiven

Its a short walk only
won't take much of your time
I've got some things to say

You're beating yourself up
but it happened long ago
there's no need to bring it up

much has changed
you have changed
you can't be blamed

your circumstance was out
of your control
you were beaten
and bruised

such wounds took a long time to heal
the point now is
to move on towards
purification

Mu

Nothingness
written on their tomb
plain for you to see
Ozu and his mother
dust into the earth

one, to decry fate
the bond of the womb
plain for you to see
did not go gentle into the night

two, to resign to fate
all for naught
darkness lies on the other side
eternity does not fit into now

a couple's bones clenching in the Vesuvius ash
your ashes will lie gentle
for short duration
Ashes to ashes
dust to dust
then disappear forever

on earth we are eight billion
but one hundred billion
have lived before

Steel Branches

Michael Martinez

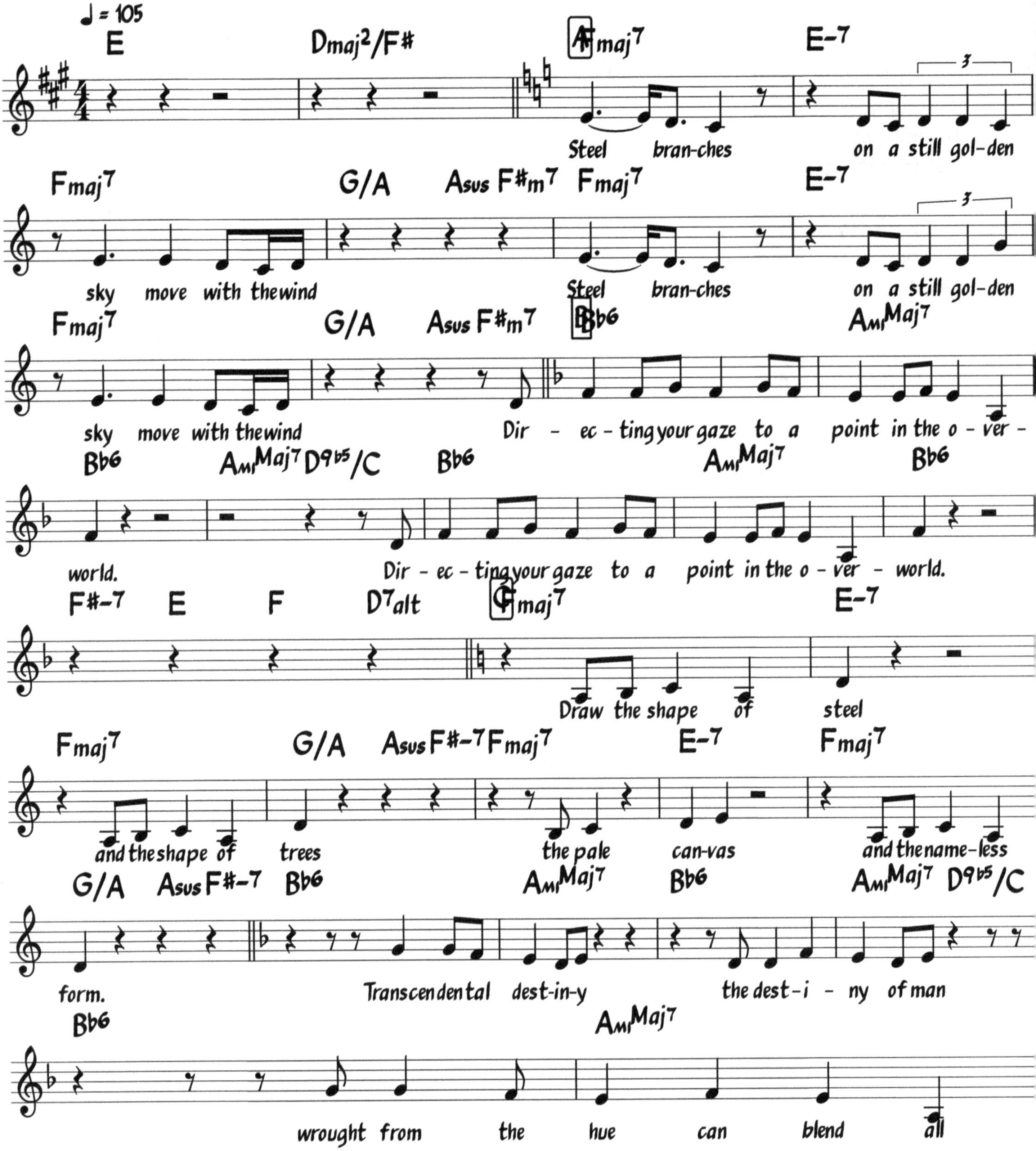

Bb6   F#-7   E   F   D7alt   [D] Fmaj7   E-7   Fmaj7

color in - to one.   sax solo

E-7   E   C#-   G#-   C#-   G#-   [E] C#-   G#-

All ob-jects burst in - to being on the

C#-   G#-   D6   F#-

the in-fin-ite mo-tion-less pal - lette.   The act of cont-rast is the

D6   G/E   C#m7b5   C#-   G#-

act   the act of ex-sis-tence.   The forming of disc - ernment.

C#-   G#-   B-7   E-7   B-7

Pri-mor-dial re - fu-sal.   Pri-mor-dial re - fu-sal.   Re-fu-sal to

E-7   F#7sus/C#

dis - si - pate.

2

Good Night, Moon

Michael Martinez

A D / A/C# / B-7

In the tran - quil night   I say ay good   night to you moon   cas - ting your pure white

A7 / D / A/F# / F#7 / G

light.   A cross al - fal - fa fields come di - i-stant soo-thing sounds   and ri - sing sweet scents to -

A7 F#7 / B-7 / A / Gmaj7

night.   I lie by my self   snug un-der co - vers,   a - lone in my room   in the

A / D-7 C G- / E-7b5 A7b13

night - time world.   Far - a - way dog barks a - cross al - fal-fa fields.

B Fmaj2 / Csus4 / Fmaj2 / Csus4

D-7 / Csus4 / D-7 / Csus4

C

High - way truck makes its   sol - i - ta - ry way through the star - ry   landscape and the

des - ert   air.   A -

mong the out - line of jag-ged top me - sas and sca - a - ttered sage-brush in a moon – lit neg–a–tive. High – way one day will take me far a-way a fut – ure un-known a

fut – ure brave night – time world of moons and stars...

It's Never Late

Michael Martinez

A C#-   E   Amaj7

Sev-en-ty with the win-dows   melt in-to the pic-ture   think-ing a-bout for-ev-er
We can't do much bet-ter   some day in our real lives   we wil real-ly live them

Bsus   B

now — — o
yeah — — eah

C#-   E   Amaj7

Sev-en-ty with the win-dows   you and me on time is   plow for our to-mor-rows
Some how we are still now   try to be a-live now   strive for some un-known thing

Bsus   B

yeah — — hh.
yeah — — hh.

B A   B   C#-   Bsus   B

Late   it's ne-ver late is now.   Too

A   B   C#-   G#-

late   it's nev-er late is now.

Too

C   Instrumental solo then to [B] then Stop.

The Forever Lament (I)

Michael Martinez

A

Li - ving in sym-bols / can't see the truth
Truth would destr-oy us / ze - ro sum game

for - e - ver con - signed to mov-ing in mists.
an - i - mal con - scious works myster-i - ous ways.

hid-den be-neath us / just be - yo - nd reach
ori - gi - nal veil / forged in bru-mal stillness.

B

since the foun - da - tion of the world. The past is
drift-ing a - midst us throuogut the ag - es. We follow the

still here the smo - ky con-fu - sion, When our
out - line the lit - uus in the sky The

C

thoughts and our dreams drift - ed to-geth - er. This is the for-
cine - ra - ry urn behind us in sha - dow.

ev - er la - ment: We know not what we do. This is the for-

ev - er la - ment.

Additional lyrics:

[A]

from the dim smoky flicker, of the first night time fire, a blind spot in our vision
to the erudite light, of the democratic age, a poetic distraction
constructing laws from veils, we have been walking sonambulent, for millenia (ages)
we wonder is Cosette lost to history, among the cyclic epochs of men

[B]

ignoring the sword leaning on the fasces
we read the language of our time
discoursing within the labyrinth of custom
is there no balance to be had, on the human scale

I Still Hide, Laura

Michael Martinez

Slow Swing

A | C | A6 | E-7 | Dmaj7

I still hide be-hind shy-ness of heart   feeze when the words come too fast

Fmaj7 | G

seek ten - der - ness   of   spi - rit

F | G | C | A6 | E-7 | Dmaj7

long for a gen - tle touch   hike up en - chan-ting rock an

Fmaj7 | G

ev' - ning stroll a - round the ci - ty

Fmaj7 | G | **B** | B | F♯ | Emaj7 | D♯-/F♯

square. Let's take it   slow let's not ven-ture far from sim-ple kindness   A

Emaj7 | F♯

walk   in   the   park

Emaj7 | F♯ G♯- | B | F♯ | Emaj7 | D♯-/F♯

Is the per-fect out-ing. Take a   stroll through the app - le or-chards of our youth.

Emaj7 | D♯-7

Dais - ies run - ning ri - ot

Emaj7 | F♯ G♯- | F♯ | Emaj7 | D♯-7 | Emaj7

in the gold-en twi-light. I still hide   in star-ry skies with tears of brum-al still-ness.

Chorus

20 D#-7 · · · · · Emaj7 · ·
Mov - ing in a trans - lu - cent

21 F# E G#- F# Emaj7 D#-7 Emaj7
world. I still hide in earn-est sor-row our e-pheme-ral lives.

24 D#-7 Emaj7
Bridge is reach - ing to me

25 F# Amaj7/B Sax break **A** C A6 3
from ac-ross for - e - ver. Let's go win-dow shop ping on

28 Dmaj7 3
Fifth Av - e - nue Let's sit on a

29 Fmaj7 G F G C A6 3 Em7
bench and watch ev - 'ry - one walk-ing by. You grew up far a-way in a

32 Em7 Dmaj7 3 Fmaj7 G F G
land of grey and cold. You like it here, the sun and warmth. The

35 Fmaj7 Em7/A B- Cmaj2 B- Cmaj2
sim - ple things are best the park is love-ly at this time of year and

38 B- Cmaj2 Fmaj7 Em7/A B- Cmaj2 B- Cmaj2
drop by for a cup of tea un - a-nnounced and al - ways wel-come.

42 B- Cmaj2 To CHORUS

2

A Juncture of Peace

Michael Martinez

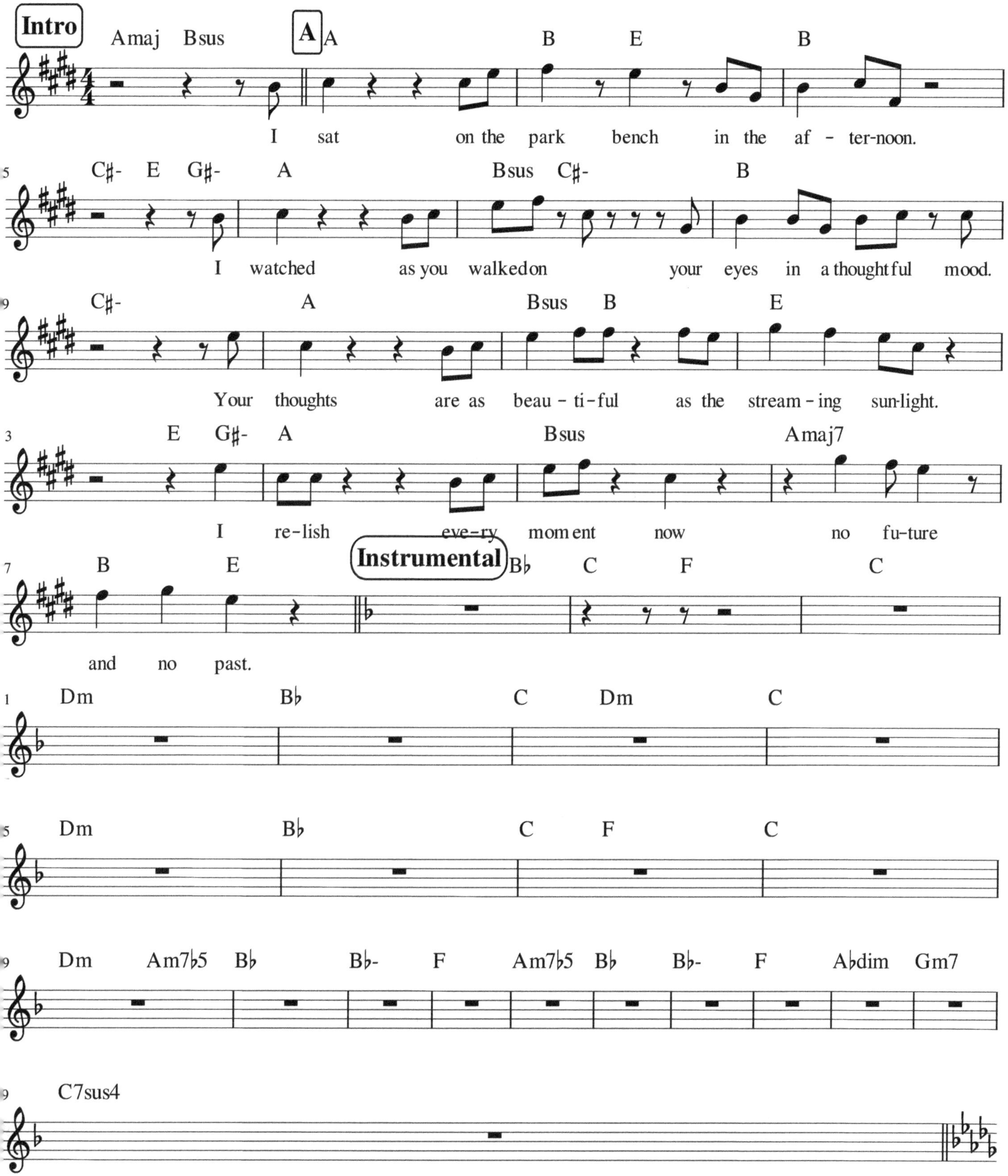

G♭maj7/D
A♭
Pour - ing down
D♭ A♭ B♭- G♭
like honey golden sun - light in this still frame lens There is no past
A♭ B♭- A♭ B♭- G♭
or fut-ure e - ter - ni-ty is fro - zen now. An old man
There is no
A♭ D♭ A♭ B♭-
strol-ling with a walk - ing cane is lost in rap-ture now.
fut-ure and no past e - ter - ni - ty is pres-ent now.
G♭ A♭ B♭- A♭
The own-er of the bask-et shop is lean-ing in
There is no fu - ture and no past, We all are bound
B♭- G♭ A♭ D♭ A♭
her door - way. You are the sub ject of this, con - tent to
to - geth - er.
B♭- G♭ A♭ B♭- A♭
watch you as you are. You are the sub ject of this im - press - ion -
B♭-
is - tic paint - ing.
Ending: sax or guitar solo over chords of verse...

Trickster

Michael Martinez

Verse 1:
The brisk stride the muf-fled hell - o The fast smile gone as you go. Your un - der - tone acc - u - sing and weak. a- ban - doned now a - ban - doned now a - ban - doned now a - ban - doned now.

Verse 2:
The mask thin but looks to be whole. The color drained out of our face. The trick ster god has turned the wheel. Lit the fuse he's lit the fuse he's lit the fuse he's lit the fuse.

One eye closed.
Droop - ing face.

Trem - ling hand.
Yell - ow skin.

Grey Skies and Blue Waters

Michael Martinez

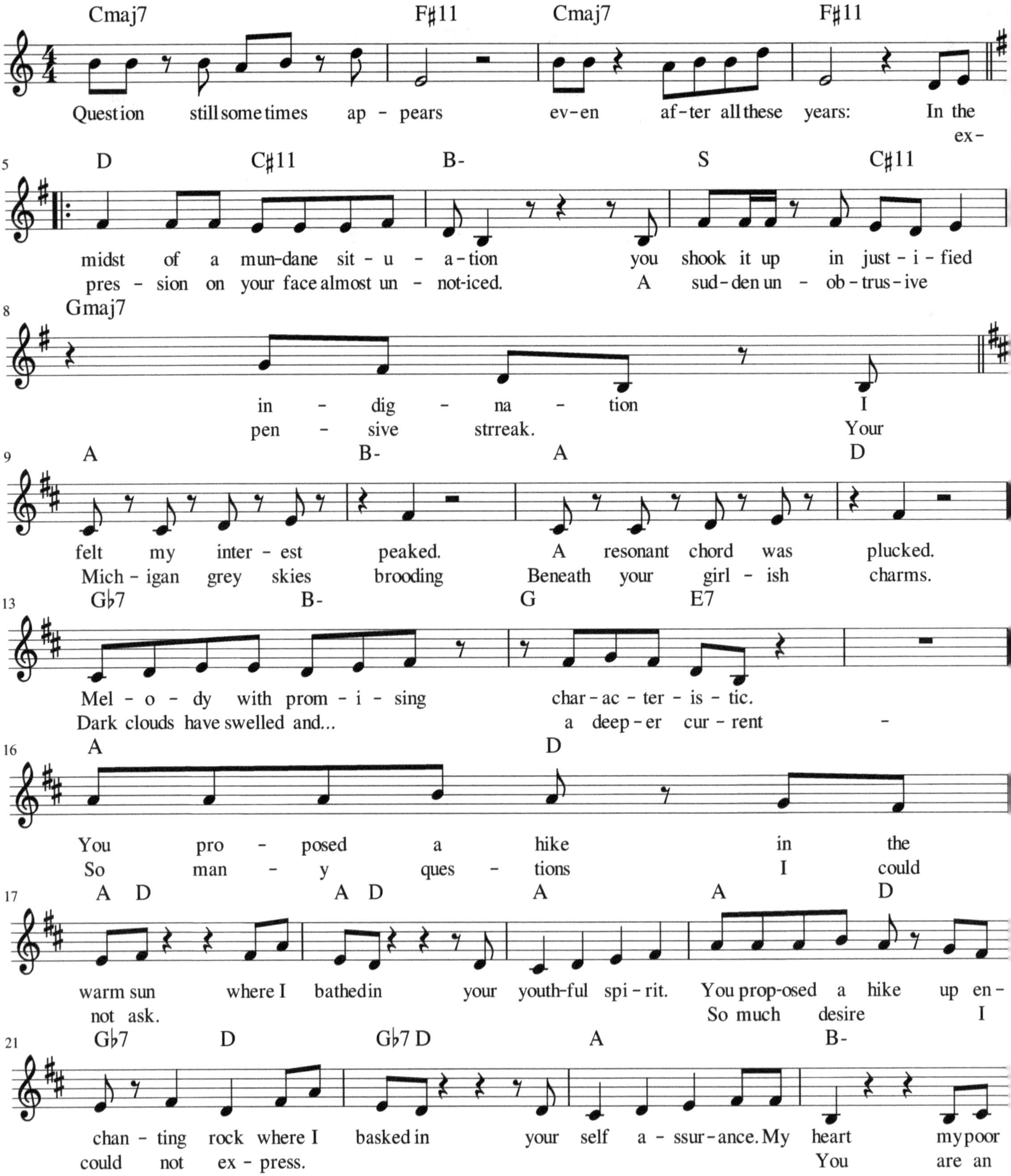

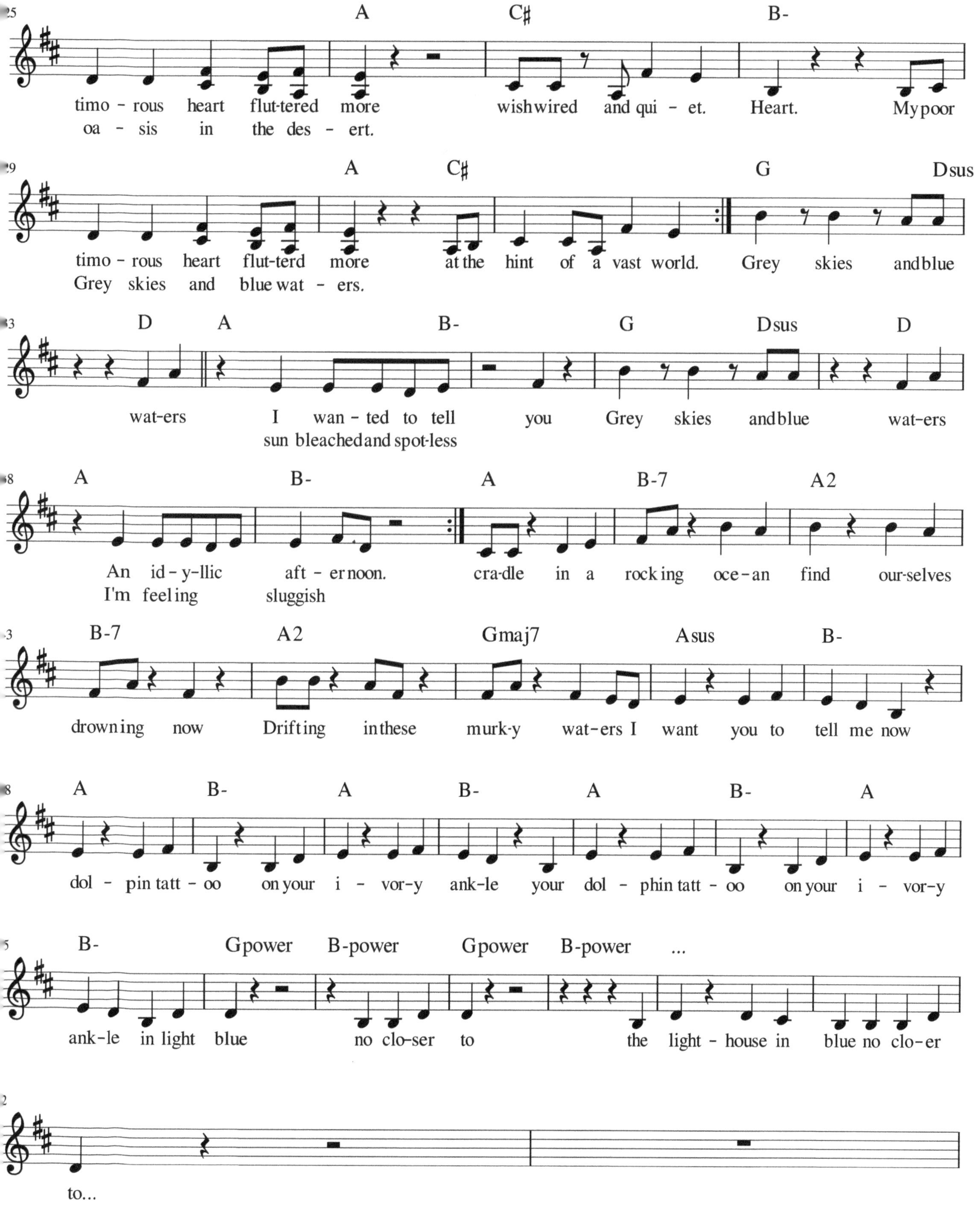
A C♯ B-
timo - rous heart flut-tered more wishwired and qui - et. Heart. My poor
oa - sis in the des - ert.
A C♯ G Dsus
timo - rous heart flut-terd more at the hint of a vast world. Grey skies and blue
Grey skies and blue wat - ers.
D A B- G Dsus D
wat-ers I wan - ted to tell you Grey skies and blue wat-ers
sun bleached and spot-less
A B- A B-7 A2
An id - y-llic aft - er noon. cra-dle in a rock ing oce - an find our-selves
I'm feel ing sluggish
B-7 A2 Gmaj7 Asus B-
drown ing now Drift ing in these murk-y wat-ers I want you to tell me now
A B- A B- A B- A
dol - pin tatt - oo on your i - vor-y ank-le your dol - phin tatt - oo on your i - vor-y
B- Gpower B-power Gpower B-power ...
ank-le in light blue no clo-ser to the light - house in blue no clo-er
to...

the single lane wanders
around the corner and upwards
into the mountain
the lamppost burns next to the shop

Eternity only has meaning for mortal things.

www.ingramcontent.com/pod-product-compliance
Lightning Source LLC
Chambersburg PA
CBHW080536030426
42337CB00023B/4760